Interior of the dye workshop at the Gobelin factory near Paris as depicted in 1763.

DYEING AND DYESTUFFS

Su Grierson

Shire Publications Ltd

CONTENTS

Set in 9 point Times roman and printed in Great Britain by C. I. Thomas & Sons (Haverfordwest) Ltd, Press Buildings, Merlins Bridge, Haverfordwest, Dyfed.

British Library Cataloguing in Publication Data: Grierson, Su. Dyeing and Dyestuffs. 1. Fabrics. Dyeing. I. Title. 746.6. ISBN 0-85263-978-3.

ACKNOWLEDGEMENTS
   The author was most generously given access to materials and information by the late Dr F. Jones at the University of Leeds, and wishes to thank Dr G. W. Taylor and Penelope Walton for constructive comments, and the following for kindly supplying photographic material: National Museums and Galleries on Merseyside, page 6; Dr V. Daniels, Department of Conservation, British Museum, page 5; Department of Colour Chemistry, University of Leeds, pages 7, 16 (lower), 24, 30 (lower); Royal Botanic Garden, Edinburgh, pages 9 (upper left), 25; Wisbech and Fenland Museum, page 9 (upper right and lower); Mr and Mrs W. Brown, Crieff, Perthshire, page 11; Jenny Balfour-Paul, pages 13 (lower), 14 (upper); Paisley College of Technology, page 17 (upper); Dumbarton District Library, page 17 (lower); Leeds Industrial Museum, page 19 (lower); Philippa Tomlinson (Environmental Archaeology Unit) and Dick Hunter (Department of Biology), University of York, page 20; Penelope Walton, York Archaeological Trust, page 21; D. J. Hackett and A. Henderson, Leeds, page 23; the late William Robertson, Comrie, Perthshire, page 26 (lower); Trustees of the Innerpeffray Library, Perthshire, page 27.

Many primitive sheep breeds had coloured fleece similar to that displayed here by a splendid ram of the Hebridean breed. Although white fleece was preferred for dyeing clear bright colours, it was not uncommon for naturally pigmented fleece to be top-dyed with a deeper colour such as brown, black or dark blue.

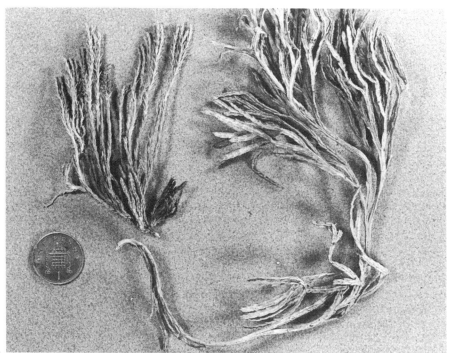

Clubmoss. Containing aluminium, these plants were used to mordant wool. (Left) Diphasiastrum alpinum, used as a mordant in rural Scotland. (Right) Lycopodium complanatum, which was much used as a mordant plant in Scandinavia.

INTRODUCTION

The history of dyeing reflects both the wonders of the natural world in supplying the colours and the ingenuity of man in discovering and perfecting the techniques of extracting and applying these colours as dyes.

Primitive people used simple stains (that is, fugitive colours that are not chemically fixed) on shells, beads, feathers and skins. Painters made pigments (colours that are fixed to the surface of an object by another adhesive medium) from both plant and mineral matter. True dyes, however, are the colours deposited on fibres, in an insoluble form, from a solution containing the colourant.

Natural dyes can be described as either *substantive* or *adjective*. The substantive group, also called 'direct' dyes, become chemically fixed to the fibre without any assistant; lichen dyes and vat dyes such as indigo are examples. Those in the adjective group, also called 'mordant' dyes, to which most dyes belong, require a metal salt to effect their permanent fixation. These metal salts are known as *mordants* and can be applied to the fibre from a solution, either along with the dye, before dyeing begins, or occasionally after dyeing is complete. Salts of aluminium and iron were the most common traditional mordants, with copper, tin and chrome coming into use later. In rural locations where mordants were not always available, plants were sometimes used for this purpose. The clubmosses that were used as mordants in northern Europe have a particular ability to accumulate aluminium.

White fibres are generally preferred for

3

dyeing, as they create the brightest colours, but fleece from sheep with natural pigmentation was also used in the past, particularly for dyeing dark or black colours. Colour variations were also achieved by adding acid or alkaline additives to the dyebath. Traditionally these were obtained from specific plants or fermented urine.

Many of the dyestuffs mentioned throughout the text are described more fully in the chapter on notable natural dyestuffs at the end of the book.

Key to plan of cover picture: A, dried weld; B, Paisley shawl; C, dried ling heather; D, jar of cochineal — whole dried beetles; E, inkle woven belt using natural dyed yarn; F, page of samples using early synthetic dyes from 'The Printing of Textile Fabrics' 1897; G, jar of cudbear; H, stems of munjeet; I, fleece dyed with seaweed (green) and lichen (gold and brown); J, Aleppo galls; K, roots of Lithospermum chrythrorhiza; L, quercitron bark; M, roots of lady's bedstraw; N, Persian berries; O, fresh henna leaves; P, illustrations of plants for dyeing in Rhind's 'History of the Vegetable Kingdom'; Q, Turkey-red printed cottons; R, modern tartan dyed with cochineal, indigo and weld. Inset: 1, combination dye using fustic, cochineal and turmeric; 2, lac/alum; 3, safflower on cotton; 4, cochineal/tin; 5, madder/alum; 6, munjeet/alum; 7, lady's bedstraw/tin, 8, Butea frondosa flowers; 9, weld top-dyed with indigo; 10, lokau on cotton; 11, blaeberries/alum on silk; 12, woad; 13, indigo on silk; 14, logwood/alum; 15, indigo top-dyed with cochineal; 16, indigo top-dyed with lichen Ochrolechia tartarea; 17, lichen Roccella crocea; 18, lichen Ochrolechia tartarea/soda; 19, lichen Ochrolechia tartarea; 20, alkanet root/alum on silk; 21, elder berries/tin on silk; 22, cochineal/copper; 23, weld/alum; 24, saffron/alum on silk; 25, Delphinium zalil/alum on silk.

The three species of shellfish used along the shores of the Mediterranean to produce the dye known as Tyrian purple. (Left upper and lower) Purpura haemastoma. (Middle upper and lower, and right upper) Murex brandaris. (Right lower) Murex trunculus.

ANTIQUITY

For at least fifteen thousand years before Christ, European man was painting himself and his cave dwellings with mineral pigments obtained from ochrous earth. His palette was limited to black and white and a range of yellow and reddish brown colours.

By the neolithic era, which in Europe was about 7000 - 2000 BC, prehistoric man was developing settlements and agriculture, and began to have notions of textile production. Spindle whorls, looms and specimens of patterned weaving have been excavated at neolithic lake dwelling sites in Europe. In order to make cloth patterns even more effective, the next step would have been to include various colours, so in Europe at some unknown date during this period the skills of dyeing must have begun.

Dye analysis carried out on various excavated textile fragments has found that woad, a blue dye that is difficult to use, along with an as yet unidentified red

dye, were in use in Denmark in the first century AD. The arrival of the Romans in north-west Europe heralded the use of new dyes and dyed textiles brought in from other parts.

In early historic times dyeing was practised throughout the world, but only the areas of greatest civilisation left written records of the skills and only areas with soil conditions particularly suitable for the preservation of textile material provide actual evidence of the use of dyestuffs.

A technical recipe book now known as the Stockholm Papyrus details the dyestuffs and dyeing techniques practised in Egypt around the third or fourth centuries AD and, together with the writings of earlier classical authors, this gives a picture of dyeing not only as practised then, but probably as it was for thousands of years previously.

Firstly, the fibres were cleaned using plant saponins (natural soap) and alka-

This fragment from a Coptic textile dating from the fourth to sixth centuries AD is woven in the dark purple colour that was fashionable in ancient Egypt. Here the medallion motif is woven in purple wool and natural-coloured linen.

line liquids made with wood ashes or stale urine. The fibres were mordanted using various mineral and plant substances; alum, copper and iron oxides, sulphur and various unidentified earths or stones were employed. Analysis of the mordant metals found in excavated textiles has shown that the dulling or 'saddening' agents of iron and tannin were frequently present in red, blue, green and purple dyes. This is not surprising as the Egyptians are known to have liked dark colours. Both tin and zinc were also unexpectedly found as mordants.

The Stockholm Papyrus recipes also indicated the refined skills used in the actual dyeing process. For example, the art of rendering soluble a most difficult dyestuff, alkanet root, was tackled in depth. No fewer than ten recipes were given, employing such aids as oil, camel's urine, natron (natural alkaline salts), purging weed, wild cucumber, fresh barley malt, vinegar, lime water, the interior of Persian nut, henbane, lentils, root of mulberry tree, root of caper bush and sheep's urine. Colour variations were obtained by dyeing the alkanet purple in combination with woad, madder, kermes and heliotrope. Excavated Coptic textiles

dated between the fourth and sixth century are largely of undyed linen with dyed wool embroidered or woven patterns. Very dark purple produced by a combination of indigo and madder was a favourite shade; yellow was produced from weld, and indigo blue was much used. Madder red is known to have been used in Egypt from the fourteenth century BC, but the insect red dyes of kermes and lac are found only on textiles of the second century AD, having arrived with other Islamic influences.

A dyeing industry which flourished in the Mediterranean before Christianity was that of Tyrian purple, the exotic purple dye produced from shellfish. Within some species of shellfish there exists a tiny sac filled with a colourless dye precursor which is converted to the final purple dye colour only after application to the fibre and exposure to sunlight and air. The shells were crushed to extract the dye.

In other parts of the world the dyers of antiquity followed different routes. In China silk was the predominant fibre and dyers developed techniques suited to that material. A Chinese text from the third millennium BC records dye processes for

6

red, black and yellow dyes. Ancient texts from India, where cotton was the major fibre, list yellow dyestuffs and red wood dyes and note the use of blue from indigo plants.

In Central and South America, where textiles were made mainly from various plant fibres, the ancient dyers used the roots of many *Relbunium* species which contain a red dyestuff similar to that of madder. In some areas red was obtained from various indigenous species of cochineal insects. The shellfish dyeing of the Mediterranean was not unique, for at a similar time the coastal Indians of Mexico were using their own *Purpura* species. By a process of blowing and tickling, these shellfish were induced to spit out the precious dye precursor directly on to the cotton fibres.

From Ireland there is archaeological evidence of dyeing with dog-whelks in the seventh century, using the native *Purpura lapillus*.

Some of these ancient dye processes are still not fully understood, yet many have continued in use until the twentieth century.

EUROPE

It is difficult to perceive the art of dyeing in Europe as one entity. Such a diversity of people, cultures and climates, together with the effects of invading forces both military and cultural, not to mention the pervading influence of fashion, resulted in a great variety of dyeing practices. Wars, revolution and religious conflict decimated many prosperous centres of dyeing, such as that of Paris in the French Revolution. Manuscripts from the eighth century onward indicate that dyers and painters were skilled in the use of native plants for colour. However, from the time that the Romans arrived in the north of Europe, dyestuffs and dyed textiles from more distant parts had also been traded northward.

Throughout Europe in the middle ages two features were of paramount importance to the art of dyeing. Firstly trade instigated by the Crusades and later promoted by the growing cultural awareness of the Renaissance, brought to the European commercial centres increasing amounts of exotic dyestuffs from the orient, and later from the Americas as well. Secondly, there was the universal desire to improve, standardise and regulate dyeing practices.

One of the major early centres for imported dyestuffs was Venice. From the beginning of the fifteenth century large quantities of brazilwood from the Far

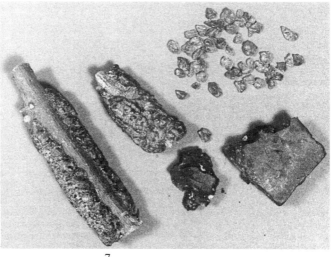

Examples of lac collected in the early twentieth century. (Left) Stick lac; the resinous insect crusts are still attached to the twigs. (Right upper) Seed lac; the broken resin has been washed free of dye and is now ready for conversion into shellac. (Right lower) The dye has been evaporated and formed into cakes for use in dyeing.

7

Crocus sativus.

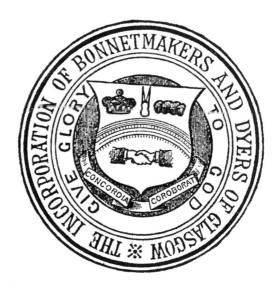

Left: *Saffron. Each saffron crocus has only three dye-bearing stamens. The yellow colour that saffron imparts has a unique golden quality which is especially beautiful on silk. It was an expensive dye even in ancient times and Pliny wrote that 'Nothing is adulterated as much as saffron.'*

Right: *Craftsmen were regulated by guilds in Egypt in the first century AD. Throughout medieval Europe guilds controlled commerce and the practices and lives of craftsmen. Because of low standards in their work dyers were sometimes incorporated with the guilds of better regulated crafts. Traditionally guilds had seals, badges and banners depicting their skills. This badge of the Incorporation of Bonnetmakers and Dyers of Glasgow included a rainbow to symbolise the dyers' colours.*

East, lac (an insect dye) and later indigo, from India, were arriving there and the dyers of Italy became highly advanced in the mastery of these dyestuffs. Written in the 1540s, the *Plictho* of the Venetian author Giovanventura Rosetti was a very early dyer's manual which included instructions for the use of both lac and indigo from Baghdad. From their port of entry into southern Europe the dyestuffs moved north to major distribution centres like Basle and Frankfurt. As an important commercial centre in the Rhine valley, Basle traded greatly with the Italians. Since the fourteenth century it had been a noted centre for trade in saffron, the expensive yellow dyestuff and medicinal herb which was obtained from the stigmas of *Crocus sativus*. Later saffron was grown as a crop in the area, becoming so important that the crocus featured on the city's coat of arms. For just such reasons the plant also gave its name to the English town of Saffron Walden. Similarly, the trade fairs which began in the twelfth century at Frankfurt, by the fourteenth century were dominated by the trade in locally grown woad. European dyers were totally dependent on the woad plant, *Isatis tinctoria*, for all substantial blue dyes before the introduction of indigo. Many regions specialised in growing woad and taking it through the complex fermentation process needed to produce the dye.

Oppressive legislation was applied to every aspect of woad growing in Germany and the dyers and woad workers were themselves closely regulated by guilds. In Frankfurt each grower brought his crop to the Guildhall, where it was tested by a 'sworn dyer' to determine its tinctorial value and officially weighed and checked before sale. Fewer restrictions were placed upon the English woad growers, who were concentrated primari-

Above: *Woad, Isatis tinctoria (formerly called Isatis sativa), was traditionally cultivated for its blue dye. Julius Caesar reported that Britons stained their bodies with woad. It was used for dyeing by ninth-century 'Viking age' people in York, and in medieval Europe guilds closely controlled all aspects of woad use. Indigo imported from the east finally superseded European woad, which was eventually used only as a fermenting agent in indigo vats.*

Above right: *Two Cambridgeshire 'waddies' balling the woad after the initial fermentation had reduced it to a pulp. These balls were air-dried on large outdoor racks.*

Above: *Mr Burnham and his horse Tom pulling the crushing roller at Parson's Drove, a woad mill near Wisbech in Cambridgeshire. Each roller weighed up to 25 cwt (1270 kg). The mill was demolished in 1914.*

ly in Somerset and Lincolnshire. A proclamation of 1587 did attempt to restrict growers to 20 acres (8 ha) each and parishes to 40 or 60 acres (16 or 32 ha), but this was repealed after two years. Another item in that proclamation did, however, continue for longer: because of the highly offensive odour emitted from woad mills, none were to be sited within 3 miles (4.8 km) of a royal residence, city or market town. This was more than just an English idiosyncrasy, for in 1413 the city of Venice had been persuaded by local doctors to prohibit dyeing with either woad or ox-blood after 1st March each year because of the unhealthy smell.

Manuscripts and illustrations have depicted workshop dye vessels used through the centuries. The drawings shown here represent some of these styles. All have a winch beam to control the descent and uplift of lengths of cloth. From left to right: fifteenth century; sixteenth century; eighteenth century; nineteenth century.

Throughout the middle ages restrictive dyeing legislation continued. In many countries dyers were graded, the master dyers using 'fast' colours only, whilst their lesser colleagues were restricted to the fugitive dyes, being forbidden even to possess, let alone use, the major dyestuffs.

The government of Spain dominated and controlled the trade in cochineal, the red dye from insects 'claimed' by her conquering forces in Central America. In 1587 approximately 65 tons of cochineal were reputedly shipped to Spain. Huge quantities of this new product went on to the north European ports, especially Hamburg. It was shunned by Italy, which was already well established in the use of the European insect dye known as kermes, and it was at first only cautiously imported into Britain. However, the intense colorific value of the cochineal dye and its comparative cheapness soon swept away all opposition and the Span-ish government clung dearly to its monopoly of this lucrative trade.

In the sixteenth and seventeenth centuries intrepid adventurers established world-wide trading posts and a shipping network traversed all the major oceans. This, together with an entrepreneurial hunger that established such trading giants as the East India Company, brought the dyestuffs of the world to the shores of Europe. Narrow legislation brought into being in earlier centuries to control and protect the growers and users of specific dyestuffs was swept aside and the first murmurings of a consumer society started to establish new requirements in terms of colour and quality.

In the eighteenth and nineteenth centuries colonialism guaranteed the supply of foreign dyestuffs, technology and industry met the challenge of large-scale production and chemists found ways of making the natural dye colours not only beautiful, but also fast to soap and light.

Simple dye vessels used for dyeing either skeins of yarn or loose fleece. (Left) An iron vessel used in rural Scotland in the nineteenth century. (Right) An ancient Chinese form of earthenware dye vessel with a twisting frame attachment.

WORKSHOPS AND VESSELS

In dye literature many terms are used to denote the receptacle in which dyeing takes place: tub, cask, pot, cauldron, copper, kettle and vat are the most common examples. In some cases the meaning is specific: for example, a copper might be made of that metal, but traditionally terminology has not been consistently employed. As a guide, however, tubs and casks were normally wooden, although possibly with a metal or slate lining; they were used as holding tanks for cold dye liquid or for hot dyeing in which the wooden bowl was heated, at a safe distance from the fire, by the circulation of hot air. Pots and cauldrons were made of iron and were suspended, or supported on short legs, directly above the fire. A copper was not always made of copper, but certainly of some metal, and often had a rounded base which was set into a brick surround or bench for support. Kettles were of various metals and were mainly used for intensive boiling of the dyestuff. The term 'vat', has often been used in a generic sense to denote any dye vessel but should refer only to the container employed in reduction dyeing, particularly of indigo, as well as to that dye process itself. The term 'indigo vat' would be taken to mean both the vessel and its contents together.

Manuscript illustrations from the middle ages show how large wooden or metal tubs were supported above the fire by brick or concrete structures. Dyers are portrayed heaving the yarn out of the dye liquor with poles, whilst cloth was turned and lifted by primitive winches placed over the dye vessel. Such simple techniques were repeated by domestic and workshop dyers in later centuries, vessels became larger and techniques were refined, but even the first industrial dyeing equipment was essentially the same as that of the previous centuries.

'Twisting poles' were a universal method of removing surplus dye or water from skeins of yarn. In China they were placed on cross pieces over the dyepot, while in Europe pegs were placed on the walls above the dye vessels.

Heating of the dyebath was a necessity that again gave rise to common solutions. Generally great heat is needed only for extracting the dye from the dyestuff, but, once the dye liquor is strained and the yarn or cloth entered, a lower continuous heat is used for most forms of dyeing. By supporting the dye vessel on a bench, plinth or legs, a strong fire can be generated beneath the vessel for the extraction process, whilst a low fire will give continued gentle heat through the circulation of hot air, often assisted by the rounded base of the vessel.

The essential procedures in dyeing have led to uniformity in workshop design throughout history and various cul-

A derelict domestic dye boiler in central Perthshire, Tayside, Scotland. Mrs Janet Brown used this boiler, which was just behind her house, until the 1940s. The round iron dyepot is set into a brick and concrete base with a fire box in front. The two side alcoves held hot coals or peat to increase the temperature at the sides and top of the pot. At the back is a tall brick chimney.

tures. In 1908 Sir W. Flinders Petrie published details of an ancient Egyptian dyeworks discovered at Athribis, dated to the Hellenistic period. Divided into two sections, the workshop had a washing area with a plentiful water supply and a dye room with sixteen vessels set into raised concrete benches. Most of these showed evidence of deep blue and red staining. The 1855 manual of a British dyer called Thomas Love outlined an ideal dyehouse of his time and this, although coming perhaps two thousand years after the construction of the Athribis workshop, was almost identical to it. He described round coppers and vats (shaped like an egg with the narrow point chopped off and with a metal flange shaped like the brim of a Quaker's hat) which were set into brick and concrete bases, cisterns for use with soap liquor, mordants and cold dye liquid, and a large water cistern. He even explained how the insides of the coppers would accumulate thick coloured crusts of dyestuff.

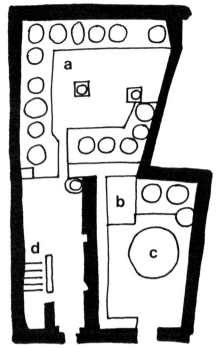

Above right: *Plan of an ancient dye workshop at Athribis in Egypt. There were two main rooms, one for washing and the other for dyeing. The dye vessels were set into cement benches, a pattern that was still used in dyeworks in eighteenth-century Europe. Key: (a) dye vessels; (b) water cistern; (c) well; (d) steps to upper floor.*

Below: *Plan of a dyehouse used for Turkey-red dyeing in the eighteenth century. The arrangement is similar to that used in ancient Egypt.*

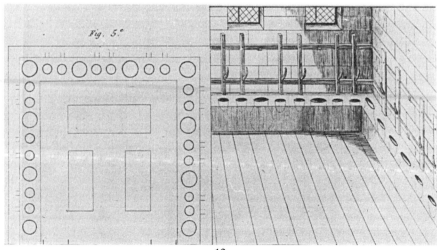

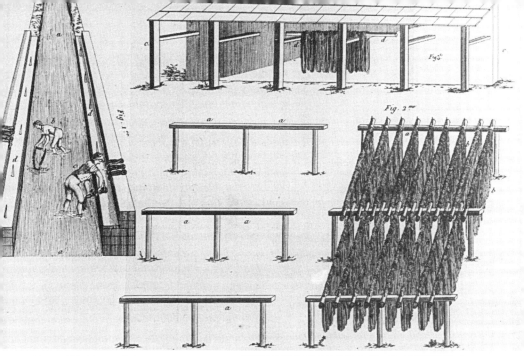

Above: *Washing and drying yarns in the late eighteenth century. The specially constructed washing lade (stream) has twisting poles for removing excess water. Yarns were dried on simple shaded and open frames.*

Right: *One of the last indigo dyers in Oman displays the tool, made from palm fronds, with which dried branches of the indigo plant are beaten in water to release the dye principle indican. The earthenware vessel, a khabiya, has a bung hole approximately 30 cm (12 inches) above the base, through which the liquid is drained. The rapidly disappearing art of indigo dyeing in South Arabia has been studied and recorded by Jenny Balfour-Paul.*

At the Beit Hakami factory in Zebid, North Yemen, cloth dyed with indigo and dipped in a starch solution is beaten with a mallet until stiff and shiny. It is also customary to enhance the colour by applying neat indigo in paste form before beating. The extremely heavy mallets are made of tamarind wood.

In the first century AD Pliny described a dye vessel kept at modest heat by means of hot air brought through flues from a distant furnace. This nineteenth-century dye vessel was kept at constant low temperature by a more modern version of that same system.

Left: *Professor Chevreul (1786-1889) worked to the end of his life of 103 years. He was superintendent at the famous Gobelin tapestry factory near Paris. Working widely in the field of organic chemistry, he isolated the dye principles of many major plant dyestuffs such as brazilwood, logwood and fustic. He published detailed works on the theory and practice of colour use.*

Right: *Professor August Wilhelm von Hofmann (1818-92) was superintendent at the Royal College of Chemistry in London and later worked in Berlin. Regarded as an outstanding chemist, he investigated coal-tar. W. H. Perkin, who discovered the first true synthetic dye, was one of his pupils. Hofmann himself produced a basic dye called Hofmann's violet in 1863.*

THE NINETEENTH CENTURY

In the nineteenth century the use of natural dyestuffs not only reached its peak but also declined almost completely.

The production of colour is just one part of the total textile-making process, the skills of spinner, designer and weaver being essential in the final display of the dyed yarns. New machinery took spinning and weaving into the realms of industry early in the nineteenth century, at a time when the equipment used by dyers was still little changed from the traditions of centuries. As textile printing and weaving technology rapidly advanced, so new demands were made on dyers. Exact shades, matched colour lots

and dyes that would withstand new mechanical and chemical processing were all demanded. Textile exporters stipulated dyes bright enough to satisfy foreign tastes and yet able to withstand tropical sunlight. Dyers in turn demanded from their suppliers chemicals of purer standards and dyestuffs of consistent quality. Dyers, dyestuff producers, chemists and manufacturers together made great technological advances as the century progressed.

Dyes of mineral origin such as Prussian blue and iron buff were already being used in calico printing by the end of the eighteenth century. Chemists in many countries developed extraction and refin-

Left: *Sir W. H. Perkin, who in 1856 at the age of eighteen had discovered the first synthetic dye.*

Below: *W. H. Perkin built this factory for the manufacture of mauveine, the first synthetic dye, in 1857 at Greenford Green near Harrow, Middlesex. As a result he made a fortune and at 35 he retired to follow pure research.*

ing processes for some major traditional dyestuffs, giving highly concentrated powders or pastes that dyed even stronger purer colours, such as cochineal carmine and madder garancine. Other procedures created indigo products that came into commerce under many names: for example, extract of indigo, sulphonated indigo, chemic and Saxon blue.

A few novel dyes, forerunners of the later synthetics, also made brief appearances, like the yellow dye obtained from picric acid. This was used at Lyons in France to create a glorious emerald-green silk dye. The blue element of this compound colour came from the exotic Chinese dye lokau, extracted from the bark of two species of buckthorn (*Rhamnus*).

In the mid nineteenth century chemistry reached new heights of enquiry. There was a universal determination to unravel the complexities of the natural world and to utilise this new knowledge

Manufactured in Scotland in the 1850s, this example of Turkey-red dyed cotton has a simple discharge pattern in red, yellow and white. These dyes were both brilliant in colour and able to withstand tropical sunlight, an essential feature since they were produced largely for export to India and the southern United States of America.

The use of madder roots in dyeing was taken to perfection by the process of Turkey-red dyeing. This lengthy and complex process fixed a brilliant red colour to cotton. Synthetic alizarin replaced madder in the late nineteenth century. The Vale of Leven in Scotland was a major centre for Turkey-red dyeing with six large dyeworks there. This aerial photograph shows the extent to which the Alexandria works had developed by the 1930s, when the old industry was finally destroyed by the arrival of new dyes.

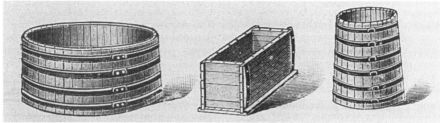

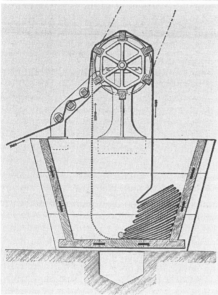

Left: The first large-scale industrial dyeing appliances were uncomplicated sophistications of traditional systems. This dye beck is no more than a wooden vessel with a mechanical winch to control the movement of the cloth through the dye liquid. A small wooden roller in the base straightened the cloth.

in conjunction with parallel developments in technology. Many new discoveries very rapidly received commercial application. The most celebrated chemist working in Europe at this time was Wilhelm von Hofmann, whose primary concern was the analysis of coal-tar. One of his students, W. H. Perkin, in an attempt to synthesise quinine, accidentally discovered the first true synthetic dye. The purple precipitate that resulted from his experiments has given the eighteen-year-old student a place in dye history. His dye, later to be called mauveine, was quickly given its first industrial application by the firm Pullars of Perth, and the young Perkin established a factory in London to produce his dyestuff commercially. In 1858, just two years after Perkins's discovery, a red aniline dye called fuchsine or magenta was patented

in France. From then until the end of the century, hardly a year passed without a major new synthetic dye being patented.

Strangely, the 'chemical' impulse that produced these totally new dyes also pushed the techniques and knowledge of the existing natural dyes to new levels of perfection. A most significant step was the introduction of chrome as a mordant. This speeded up the dye process and gave increased depth of colour. The oxidising properties of chrome made it particularly useful with logwood, which responds to oxidation for the final development of its colour. Indeed, because of the intense and pure black colours produced in this way, this form of black dyeing continued in use into the twentieth century.

One by one the dyestuffs of the old order gave way to the new arrivals. It happened unevenly, with inevitable pockets of resistance, but the trend was irreversible. Some very surprising survivals did occur, however. Lichen purple, the most fugitive of all natural dye colours, found use as a top-dye for some synthetics, adding an element of beauty to the harshness of the new colours. As

Published in 1860, this illustration shows a mechanical dye beck in use for yarn dyeing. Progressive dyehouses were at this time using some of the new synthetic dyes as well as technological improvements.

The wool dyehouse at Whitehall Mills in Leeds, as depicted in the early twentieth century. Here wool was normally dyed either as washed fleece or as cloth, and traditional methods were apparently still in use.

litmus, this dye also had a continued use for laboratory indicator papers. Generally, although some domestic dyeing continued with the use of natural dyes (notably the Scottish Hebridean tweed industry), by the end of the nineteenth century the use of synthetic dyes was firmly established. The scientific and computerised dyeing techniques of the twentieth century, born from these nineteenth-century developments, have created a totally new industry. Many problems are the same — matched colour lots and fastness still cause dyers concern — but for the first time in the history of dyeing the solutions are entirely new.

Minute plant fragments found within archaeological sites can provide information about the former use of dyeplants. Exhaustive sieving and microscope analysis by botanists at the Environmental Archaeology Unit at York University have revealed fragments of the dyeplants dyer's greenweed (Genista tinctoria), which dyes yellow, and woad (Isatis tinctoria), which dyes blue, in excavations of deposits from the ninth and tenth centuries at York. Microscope photographs show (above) a fragment of a leaf from Genista tinctoria; note the hairs along the leaf margin with scattered stomata just visible; (below) almost all that is left of a woad leaf after it had been used in the dye process.

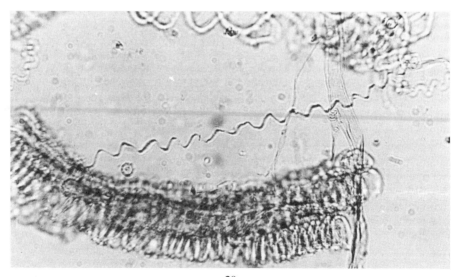

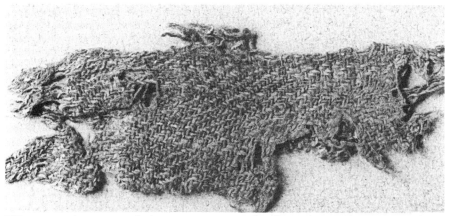

This seventeenth-century textile fragment was excavated at Newcastle-upon-Tyne. The sample was comprehensively examined by the textile analyst Penelope Walton, who found it to be dyed with madder (Rubia tinctoria), having been woven in red and cream-coloured stripes. This sample is in good condition compared with many excavated fragments, but the painstaking work involved in their analysis is essential for greater knowledge about the former use of textile dyes.

THE TWENTIETH CENTURY

Today the use of natural dyes on a commercial scale barely exists. Current worries about health aspects of some synthetic food and surgical dyes have caused a limited revival of commercial interest in turmeric, annatto, cochineal and logwood. Some very remote peoples without access to modern dyes, or with particular incentives for retaining ancient customs, do continue with traditional dye use. In Scotland, the Hebridean islands have perhaps three dyers who continue to dye traditional tweed yarn. In Africa, Japan and south Arabia, indigo dyeing has dwindled and is now used only for textiles for tourists and a select local market.

Natural dyes are not without a future, however. Craft dyeing offers a unique contact with the plant kingdom to those who are willing to accept the restraints of conservation needs. Natural dyes have been deliberately reintroduced into local carpet manufacture in Turkey and tapestry schools in Egypt.

There is also renewed scientific and historic interest in natural dyestuffs. Knowledge about their former use helps us to comprehend the daily lives of previous civilisations and, to this end, new technology can help identify dyestuffs in both archaeological material and old textiles. Understanding rates of fading and degradation is important for the future preservation of dyed textiles in museums. Whilst the dyeing industry of today keeps pace with modern science, the future use of natural dyes will also follow a new path, but one firmly rooted in tradition.

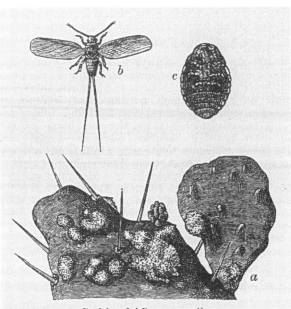

Cochineal (*Coccus cacti*):
a, living on cactus (*Opuntia*); *b*, male; *c*, female.

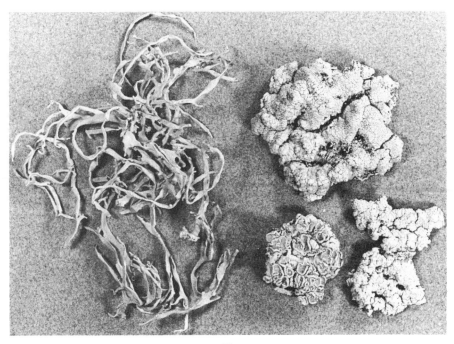

22

Cudbear was a commercially produced dyestuff made from lichens. It gave a beautiful but fugitive purple dye which was used primarily to give lustre and shading to other dyes such as indigo blue and madder red. In Leeds the firm of Yorkshire Chemicals Limited is still bounded by Cudbear Street, a reminder of the former cudbear producers John Marshall, whose works were sited there in the late nineteenth century.

NOTABLE NATURAL DYESTUFFS

Lists of the dyes used in various cultures can show the colour ranges available, as well as indicating the degree of sophistication necessary for their application. For example, the use of madder root or related dyes would indicate a knowledge of mordant dyeing, whilst the use of indigo would have required mastery of complex reduction techniques.

Many dyestuffs from around the world are fascinating for both the history and manner of their use, and the selected alphabetical listing that follows gives some examples.

Acacia: tannin, from the red heartwood of *Acacia catechu* and sold as catechu, was used for black dyeing on cotton and silk. An extract was marketed as Pegu. Gum arabic, whilst not itself a dye, was produced from *Acacia arabica* and was a vital assistant for dyeing in the European calico industry.

Alder: the tannin-rich bark of the native European tree *Alnus glutinosa* was used throughout Europe with an iron mordant for black dyes on wool. Rural dyers used alder with iron dust collected from the grinding wheel.

Alkanet: *Alkanna tinctoria* is native to the warmer parts of Europe. A purple dye, insoluble in water but soluble in many oily substances, is produced from the root. An ancient dyestuff but never a major dye, it is pH sensitive with poor lightfastness.

Annatto: the pulp surrounding the ripe seeds of *Bixa orellana* produces a dye known variously as annatto, rocou, bixin and orlean. Native to Central and South America, it was introduced to the Far East. Flag annatto was a commercial paste extract wrapped in banana leaves. A fugitive orange dye, it was used as a ground for other colours. Extensively used for colouring butter and cheese, it is barely soluble in water, but soluble in caustic alkali.

Bedstraw: a red dye exists in the roots of *Galium verum*. It grows abundantly in Scotland and has a long tradition of rural use. A mordant dye, tinctorially comparable to madder red.

Butea: the bright red flowers of the tropical climber *Butea frondosa* contain an almost colourless dye principle called butin. When steeped in cold water the butin converts to the orange dyestuff butein. Butea was used in India for a vivid but fugitive orange colour.

Brazilwood: this dye came primarily from the tree *Caesalpinia sappan*. Used in medieval Europe, it was at that time imported from Asia but was later discovered growing in South America. The wood was rasped and fermented to convert the dye principle brasilin into the dyestuff brasilein through oxidation. The red/purple dye is soluble in water but reacts to changes in pH. Other related trees give similar dyes and are known as the 'soluble' red wood dye group.

Chay: *Oldenlandia umbellata* roots were extensively used for cotton dyeing in India. Known as Indian madder it gave the normal mordant madder shades but possessed only half the tinctorial value of madder.

Cochineal: a dye made from insects from Central America, where they thrived on *nopal* cacti. Intensively traded, it was also subject to fraudulent adulterations. By using a full range of mordants and additives, colours ranging from grey/violet through carmine to full scarlet are available. The Gobe-

A page from the large leather-bound record book of Dr William Lauder Lindsay, superintendent of a mental asylum in Perth between 1856 and 1879. He was a prodigious writer and enlightened pioneer on the treatment of insanity, and also a respected lichenologist. His concern for the plight of the poor led him to study the economic potential of lichens, particularly in dyeing, believing that this could create employment in rural areas. His studies on dye lichens are still a standard source of information on the subject.

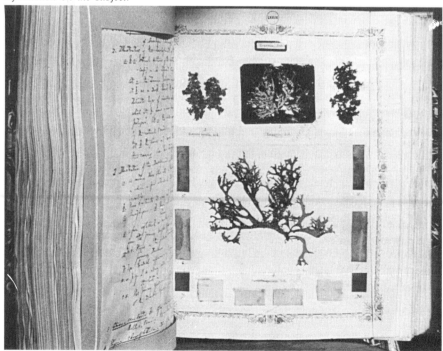

lin factory near Paris and the Bow dyeworks near London were renowned for scarlet dyeing using cochineal with tin mordant.

Cudbear: a manufactured purple dye product produced by the 'fermentation' of various lichens. Made in Scotland and England, the native lichens used were *Ochrolechia tartarea* and *Umbilicaria pustulata.* The similar products litmus and orseille, mostly made in Europe, used lichens of the *Roccella* species as well as some native lichens.

Delphinium: yellow flowers of *Delphinium zalil* and *Delphinium saniculae* were used to produce a beautiful yellow dye on silk in Persia and the Middle East. Blue-flowered delphiniums have been used for a blue dye, a cold extract from the crushed petals being applied directly to vegetable fibres.

Elder: berries of dwarf elder, *Sambucus ebulus,* and black elder, *Sambucus nigra,* were used as a rural dye in Europe. Cold crushed berries give a blue dye to linen. Violet is obtained by a hot dye on wool with alum mordant.

Fungus: some fungi have been used historically for black dyeing because of their tannin content. Modern craft workers in America, Norway and Denmark have examined fungi dyes, some of which also give orange, red and blue colours.

Galls: Aleppo galls mainly from Syria were employed in calico printing and dyeing in Europe. They were high in tannin content but light in weight for transport.

Genista: the flowering tops of *Genista tinctoria* were used for a yellow wool dye on alum. It was used in the English Lake District, particularly with indigo, to produce the dye known as Kendal green.

Heather: in the Hebrides the ling heather *Calluna vulgaris* was used as a yellow tweed dye.

Henna: an ancient brown dye produced from the leaves of *Lawsonia inermis.* Noted as a hair and fingernail dye, it required acid to develop the colour fully.

Indigo has been extracted from an estimated forty plant species worldwide. The term 'anil' was widely used for many indigo plants. This drawing made in 1718 is almost certainly of the American species Indigofera suffruticosa.

Indigo: a strong blue dye produced largely from the leaves of *Indigofera tinctoria.* The dye was produced as a powder or cake by a lengthy process of steeping and stirring. To apply the dye to cloth, indigo must be rendered soluble in an alkaline liquid containing a reducing agent. This process of 'reduction dyeing' is called vatting and in this state the indigo transforms to a 'white' form. Dyeing is carried out in the 'white' vat liquid and, after dyeing, is converted back to the blue state by exposure to atmospheric oxygen. The colourant in indigo is the same as that in woad.

Left: *The production of some major dyestuffs used in European industry supported whole communities in distant countries. This photograph taken in the 1920s shows the collection of lac insects in Thailand. The branches covered with resinous encrustations of the insect eggs were cut down and taken to the village for separation.*

Below: *Madder (Rubia tinctoria), a plant with perennial root and annual stalks. The square-stemmed stalks are straggly and can reach 8 feet (2.4 metres) in length in good soil. The leaves form whorls of four to six around the stem joints. Madder does not flower until the third or fourth year of growth. The flowers are followed by berries.*

In the early eighteenth century Philip Miller, gardener to the Worshipful Company of Apothecaries at the Botanic Garden in Chelsea, London, advocated the reintroduction of madder cultivation in Britain. From the eighth edition of his 'Gardener's Dictionary' published in 1768 comes this illustration of a grinding mill for crushing and grinding madder roots.

Kermes: a red insect dye much used in Europe before the introduction of cochineal. Obtained from the insect *Kermes vermilio*.

Lac: an insect dye from India and South-east Asia. The resinous encrustations of this scale insect provided shellac as well as the red dyestuff. An ancient dye in India.

Logwood: the wood of the tree *Haematoxylon campechianum* was imported to Europe from Central America. It was rasped and fermented before use. Although it can give good blue shades, these fade badly. Logwood was much used industrially for making an excellent black wool dye with chrome mordant.

Madder: *Rubia tinctoria* was extensively cultivated in Holland, France, Italy, Turkey and, for a period, in Britain for the red dye obtained from the roots. With different mordants it yields red, brown and purple shades.

The major dye principle is alizarin, but it contains up to nineteen different dye elements. A commercial extract of madder was marketed as garancine.

Munjeet: *Rubia cordifolia* is a small Indian creeper. The roots and lower stems give a madder-type dye known as munjeet.

Quercitron: an American dye wood from the tree bark of *Quercus tinctoria*. Imported to England in the 1770s, it went on to become a major yellow dyestuff. Used greatly with other dyes for compound shades.

Relbunium: as many as 25 species of *Relbunium* occur in South America. The roots of many of these plants produce madder-like dyes that were used by ancient civilisations in Peru and Argentina.

Safflower: this ancient but fugitive dye was extracted from the petals of *Carthamus tinctoria*. A poor yellow dye must be washed from the petals

An eighteenth-century workshop in France in which cotton yarns were taken through the numerous steepings and dyeing required to produce the bright madder dye called Turkey red.

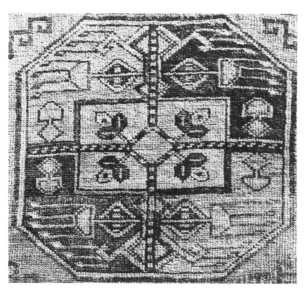

The construction of large and beautiful textiles required thousands of hours of labour in spinning and dyeing, weaving and finishing. Such textiles were made to last for many generations and required dye colours that could last for the lifetime of the textile. For this reason dyes of great permanence and lasting beauty, such as the madder and indigo used on this Turkoman rug, were used in all parts of the world.

first, then a strong pink can be extracted into an alkaline solution. Used in ancient Egypt and China. Also used in calico printing.

Saffron: each flower of the crocus *Crocus sativus* produces just three dye-bearing stamens, thus saffron was always an expensive dyestuff. Used as a dye in antiquity and as a silk dye in many parts of the world.

Seaweed: a fine green dye can be produced from the seaweed *Cladophora rupestris*, especially when used with a copper mordant. The only seaweeds recorded as ancient dyestuffs are some red species, notably *Ceramium rubrum*, *Plocamium cartilaginium* and

SAFFLOWER

Right: *Safflower, Carthamus tinctoria. The dried florets constitute the dyestuff which provides a fugitive yellow dye which is generally washed away with water and discarded before a red/pink dye is extracted in an alkaline solution. Traditionally a dye for cotton and silk, it was imported to Britain from China, India and Turkey.*

Below: *Purpura lapillus, the British dog-whelk which contains a gland capable of producing a purple dye.*

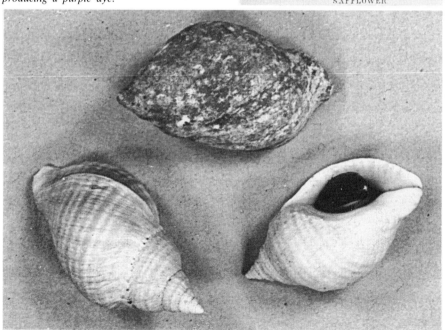

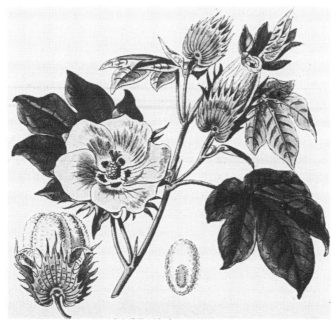

Cotton. Plants of the Gossypium species provide a major textile fibre in many parts of the world. In India the cotton blossoms were sometimes used locally as a yellow dye.

Peori. In India the toxic leaves of the mango tree were at one time fed to cattle. The resulting bright yellow urine was collected and evaporated and the residual yellow paste was dried and formed into balls which varied between 2.5 and 15 cm (1-6 inches) in diameter. Peori was used for painting buildings and as a poor textile dye and at one time it was favoured by European artists as a pigment. The process was eventually made illegal.

30

Rhytiphlea tinctoria. These are described in ancient texts as 'marine fucus'.

Tokio purple: a purple dye similar to alkanet, produced in Japan from the root of *Lithospermum chrythrorhiza.*

Turmeric: an intensely coloured substantive but very fugitive orange/yellow dye. Used extensively in India and China from an early date. The dye came from the roots of *Curcuma longa* and *Curcuma zedoaria.*

Weld: a major yellow dye in Europe. The flower spikes of the native *Reseda luteola* were used with alum. It was frequently used for green in combination with indigo or woad blue.

Woad: in Europe the leaves of *Isatis tinctoria* provided the only blue dye of substance prior to the introduction of indigo in the seventeenth century. Like indigo, the plant was subjected to complex fermentation and extraction procedures and for dyeing was generally brought to a reduced soluble state by means of a fermentation vat.

Rhamnus utilis. The bark of both Rhamnus utilis and Rhamnus chlorophorus was used in China to produce an exotic and costly dyestuff known as lokau. In France this was applied with picric acid to create a brilliant green silk dye called 'vert Venus'.

FURTHER READING

Balfour-Paul, Jenny. 'Indigo : An Arab Curiosity and its Omani Variations', in B. Pridham (editor), *Oman: Economic, Social and Strategic Developments*, Croom Helm, 1987.

Balfour-Paul, Jenny. 'Indigo and South Arabia', *The Journal for Weavers, Spinners and Dyers*, 139 (1986).

Brooklyn Botanic Gardens booklets. *Dye Plants and Dyeing*, 1964. *Natural Plant Dyeing*, 1973.

Brunello, Franco. *The Art of Dyeing in the History of Mankind*. Cleveland, Ohio, 1973.

Casselman, Karen Leigh. *Craft of the Dyer: Colour from Plants and Lichens of the Northeast*. Toronto, 1980.

Ciba Reviews. There are many dye-related issues in this series; for full list see Ponting below.

Forbes, R. J. *Studies in Ancient Technology*, volume 4. Leiden, 1964.

Fraser-Lu, S. *Indonesian Batik: Processes, Patterns and Places*. Oxford University Press, 1986.

Gittinger, Mattiebelle. *Master Dyers to the World : Technique and Trade in Early Indian Dyed Cotton Textiles*. Washington, 1982.

Goodwin, Jill. *A Dyer's Manual*. Pelham Books, 1982.

Grierson, Su. *The Colour Cauldron : The History and Use of Natural Dyes in Scotland*. Mill Books, 1986.

Hurry, J. B. *The Woad Plant and Its Dye*. Oxford, 1930.

Lawrie, L. G. *A Bibliography of Dyeing and Textile Printing*. London, 1949.

National Museums of Scotland. *Dyes on Historical and Archaeological Textiles*. 1982, 1983, 1984, 1985, 1986.

Polakoff, Claire. *African Textiles and Dyeing Techniques*. Routledge and Kegan Paul, 1982.

Ponting, K. G. *A Dictionary of Dyes and Dyeing*. Mills and Boon, 1980. Contains useful bibliography.

Rhind, William. *A History of the Vegetable Kingdom*. London, 1868.

Robinson, Stuart. *A History of Dyed Textiles*. Studio Vista, 1969.

Robinson, Stuart. *A History of Printed Textiles*. Studio Vista, 1969.

Seagroatt, Margaret. *Coptic Weaves*. Merseyside County Museums, undated.

Slater, J. W. *The Manual of Colours and Dye Wares*. London, 1882.

Wickens, Hetty. *Natural Dyes for Spinners and Weavers*. Batsford, 1983.

Wills, N. T. *Woad in the Fens*. Long Sutton, 1979.

PLACES TO VISIT

Generally the subject of dyeing seems to be poorly served by museums, but many folk life and local museums carry small relevant displays about dyes or dyeing. Intending visitors are advised to find out the opening times before making a special journey.

Colour Museum, 82 Grattan Road, Bradford, West Yorkshire BD1 2JB. Telephone: 0274 390955. There is a display on the Turkey-red dyeing industry and a very small display on natural dyestuffs. The museum otherwise deals largely with the development of modern technology and the science of dyeing and colour. A most interesting and informative museum.

Highland Folk Museum, Duke Street, Kingussie, Inverness-shire PH21 1JG. Telephone: 05402 307. Small display of native dyes and some archive material.

Scottish Tartan Museum, Davidson House, Main Street, Comrie, Perthshire. Telephone: 0764 70779. Small relevant display and dye garden at the museum. Large archive collection of early tartans which can be seen by prior arrangement only.

Wisbech and Fenland Museum, Museum Square, Wisbech, Cambridgeshire PE13 1ES. Telephone: 0945 583817. Small display on woad, some archive material.